A LIFE
WORTH LIVING

*My values, memories,
goals, and dreams*

Regena Kay Epperson Weber
Name

Beyond Words Publishing, Inc.
20827 N.W. Cornell Road, Suite 500
Hillsboro, Oregon 97124-9808
503-531-8700
1-800-284-9673

Proofreader: Marvin Moore
Design : Principia Graphica
Managing editor: Kathy Matthews

Printed in Hong Kong
Distributed to the book trade by Publishers Group West

Library of Congress Catalog Card Number: 98-73017
ISBN: 1-885223-91-9

The corporate mission of Beyond Words Publishing, Inc.:
Inspire to Integrity

E ach of our lives is unique, and regardless of our individual achievements or challenges, each of our lives is an adventure—a life worth living.

This book is intended to provide you with an easy and enjoyable way to record your life's experiences, highlights, goals, and opinions as you go along. It will probably sit on a shelf most of the time, *but you should always know where it is*. Don't feel intimidated by it. This book is yours, so don't be afraid to use it. Watch for the special and favorite things in your life, then every so often take this book down and make some notes in it.

Imagine the value of having similar books that your parents or grandparents or great-grandparents had used and passed along to you! You would very likely discover all kinds of fascinating and meaningful things about them, and you would treasure those books and pass them lovingly on to your children. You wouldn't care about the writers' spelling or whether they wrote in complete sentences or accomplished "great things" in their lives. Just learning how they spent an average day would be an eye-opening way to get to know them. You could find out what their likes and dislikes were, what work they did, what their favorite books were, what they believed in. Even the littlest, seemingly trivial things would be priceless.

Look through this book and become familiar with the subjects and the layout. There are pages for photographs and mementos and a pocket to hold letters and other documents and keepsakes. Use the book however you wish. You could include birth announcements or old pay stubs or theater tickets or whatever else you can think of.

Try to answer some or all of the questions in this book, and if for whatever reason you can't write in it yourself, *get someone to help you*. This will accomplish the same thing.

Date your entries so you can see growth and change. If you need more space, continue your comments on the open pages provided.

If in five or ten years you have entered only a few things into this book, that's better than nothing. And if you have filled it with notes and who knows what all, that's better yet. Just use it. It's been designed to be as simple and usable as possible, so *do* it! Later you will be glad that you did, and so will your family and friends. It's the most personal and special gift you could give them: a glimpse of you and your life—a life worth living.

Have fun with it!

Jerry Hawley

INTRODUCTION

Regena Kay Epperson Weber

June 10, 1954
Date of Birth

Auburn Nebraska
Place of Birth

Hair Color

Green
Eye Color

5'2"
Height

Average Weight

Stanwood, Washington
Current Place of Residence

MYSELF

W Where did you live while growing up?

What did you like or dislike about it?

Where else have you lived?

_____

_____

_____

_____

_____

_____

_____

_____

_____

Do you remember the addresses?

_____

_____

_____

_____

_____

_____

_____

_____

_____

When you were a child, what did you dream of being when you "grew up"?

Did your vision change over time? How?

What games or activities did you enjoy as a kid?

D Did you prefer to play with other kids or by yourself?

W What were your favorite classes in school?

_____

_____

_____

_____

_____

_____

_____

_____

_____

_____

_____

Your least favorite?

_____

_____

_____

_____

_____

_____

_____

_____

_____

_____

_____

_____

MYSELF

W What did you do during school holidays and summers?

hat are your most vivid memories of your childhood and teenage years?

W What were the hairstyles, clothing, and fads from your teenage years?

What was your style like?

What was your education?

_____

_____

_____

_____

_____

_____

_____

_____

_____

_____

_____

_____

_____

_____

_____

_____

_____

_____

_____

_____

_____

_____

_____

_____

Who was the most influential teacher in your life?

What impact did that teacher have on you?

Who else has influenced you?

W What helped or hindered your ability to further your education?

D Did you ever study any foreign languages? Which?

Can you still write, speak, or read them with fluency?

Would you rather live in a big city, in a small town, or in the country?

_____

_____

_____

_____

_____

Why? _____

_____

_____

_____

_____

_____

_____

_____

_____

_____

_____

_____

_____

W What do you consider to be some of your best and worst habits or traits?

How important is having a good sense of humor to you?

_____
_____
_____
_____
_____
_____
_____
_____
_____
_____

How has it helped or hindered you?

_____
_____
_____
_____
_____
_____
_____
_____
_____

Do you consider yourself to be a romantic?

Why?

Do you consider yourself to be an optimist or a pessimist?

Why?

When in your life have you felt the happiest?

Why?

W When have you felt the saddest?

_____

_____

_____

_____

_____

Why? _____

_____

_____

_____

_____

_____

_____

_____

_____

_____

_____

_____

_____

W What is the biggest fear you have conquered in your life?

_____

_____

_____

_____

_____

_____

_____

_____

_____

_____

_____

Are there still any fears that you would like to overcome?

_____

_____

_____

_____

_____

_____

_____

_____

_____

_____

What types of cars or other vehicles have you owned?

Years owned	Make	Cost

Is there one car you wish you still owned?

W What is your medical history? (Include any allergies or hereditary conditions.)

PHOTO

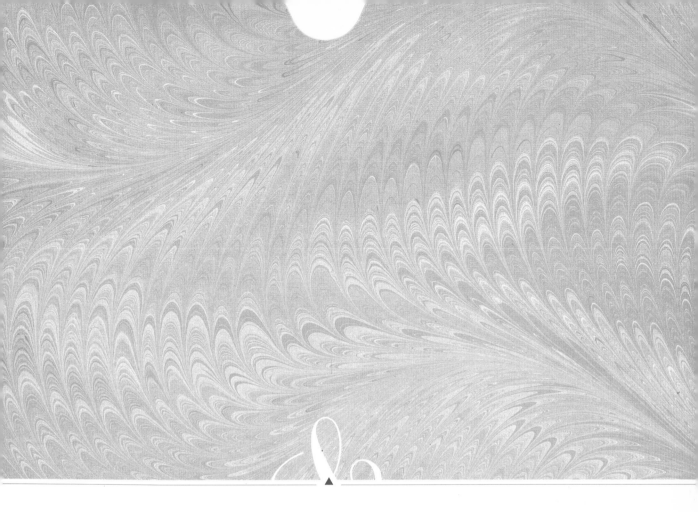
MEMENTOS
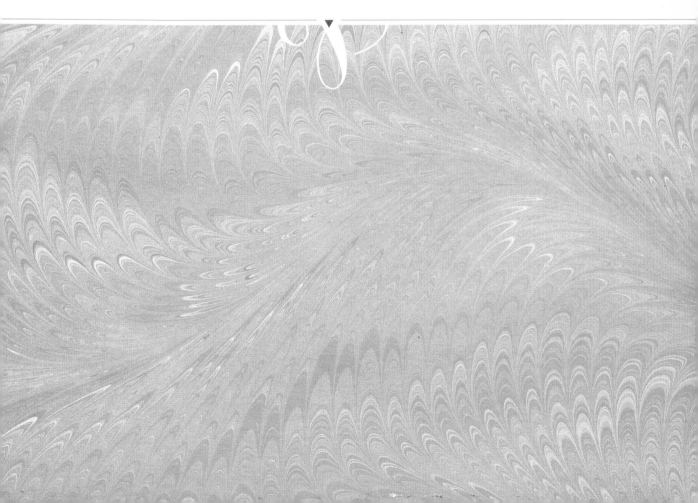

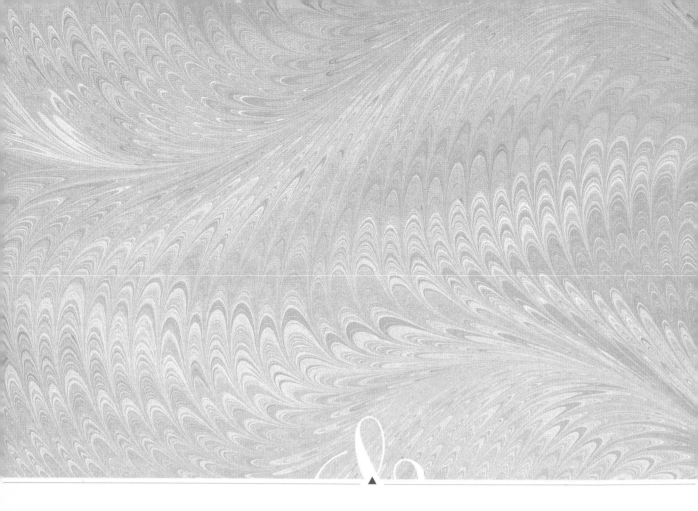

MEMENTOS

PEOPLE IN MY LIFE

How far back can you trace your ancestry?

Do you know what countries your ancestors came from?

Family Tree

4 Claude Eppers[on]
Born
Where
Married
Where
Died
Where

Harold
Ellen
Loretta
Lois
Irma
Everett

2 Leo Calvin Epperson
Born 11·4·
Where
Married 10-12
Where
Died
Where

5 Loretta Madge Well[ing]
Born
Where
Died
Where

1 Regena Kay Epperson
Born June 10, 1954
Where Auburn, Nebraska
Married April 28, 1973
Where Oregon City, Oregon
Died
Where

Allan Dale Weber
Name of Husband or Wife

6 Harry Rockwell
Born
Where
Married
Where
Died
Where

3 Rachel Eugeneie Rockwell
Born
Where
Died
Where

7
Born
Where
Died
Where

8

Born
Where
When Married
Died
Where

9

Born
Where
Died
Where

10

Born
Where
When Married
Died
Where

11

Born
Where
Died
Where

12

Born
Where
When Married
Died
Where

13

Born
Where
Died
Where

14

Born
Where
When Married
Died
Where

15

Born
Where
Died
Where

16

Born
Died

17

Born
Died

18

Born
Died

19

Born
Died

20

Born
Died

21

Born
Died

22

Born
Died

23

Born
Died

24

Born
Died

25

Born
Died

26

Born
Died

27

Born
Died

28

Born
Died

29

Born
Died

30

Born
Died

31

Born
Died

What were their accomplishments?

W What kind of work did they do?

_____
_____
_____
_____
_____
_____
_____
_____
_____
_____

What was their religion?
_____
_____
_____
_____
_____
_____
_____
_____
_____
_____
_____

Do you have any old family portraits and snapshots? Who are the people in them? How are these people related to you?

PHOTO

Do you have any family heirlooms? What is the history of them?

_____

_____

_____

_____

_____

_____

_____

_____

_____

_____

_____

_____

_____

_____

_____

_____

_____

_____

_____

How important was your family to you when you were growing up?

W What recollections do you have of parents, grandparents, great-grandparents, and other relatives?

Parents

_____

_____

_____

_____

_____

Grandparents

_____

_____

_____

_____

Great-grandparents

_____

_____

_____

_____

Other relatives

_____

_____

_____

_____

_____

Which of your relatives, if any, are you most like?

W Who were (or are) your favorite relatives? Why?

_____

_____

_____

_____

_____

_____

_____

_____

_____

_____

_____

_____

_____

_____

_____

_____

_____

_____

_____

_____

_____

_____

How often did your family have special dinners or get-togethers?

_____

_____

_____

_____

_____

_____

_____

_____

_____

_____

_____

_____

_____

_____

_____

_____

_____

_____

_____

_____

_____

_____

H How did your family celebrate holidays when you were growing up?

Have things changed? How?

Do you remember your first crush or true love?

H Have you been married?

_____
_____
_____
_____

What have been your most memorable experiences with marriage?

_____
_____
_____
_____
_____
_____
_____
_____
_____
_____
_____
_____
_____
_____
_____
_____

Do you have children and grandchildren? What are their names and birth dates? What memories do you have of them?

_____

_____

_____

_____

_____

_____

_____

_____

_____

_____

_____

_____

_____

_____

_____

_____

_____

_____

_____

_____

W What has your experience with your family been like?

_____

_____

_____

_____

_____

_____

_____

_____

_____

*Have things changed over the years? How?*_____

_____

_____

_____

_____

_____

_____

_____

_____

What special relationships have you had with parents, aunts and uncles, cousins, and other relatives?

Have you created any new traditions of your own?

Who have been your best and oldest friends?

_____

_____

_____

_____

_____

_____

_____

_____

_____

_____

What have been some of your most memorable or exciting experiences together?

_____

_____

_____

_____

_____

_____

_____

_____

_____

PHOTO

PHOTO

Do you still keep in touch with childhood friends?

Grade school friends

Junior high school friends

Theresa Gottlieb Boll Sepmeyer

High school friends

H Have you had any pets?

_____

_____

_____

_____

Pets	Names

Which were your favorite pets? _____

_____

_____

_____

PHOTO

HOW I SPEND MY TIME

What was your first real job?

How did you get it?

Do you remember the year and how much you were paid?

W

What other work have you done?

_____

_____

_____

Job	Employer	Years

Which jobs were the most enjoyable?

Which jobs were the worst?

Have you taken an extended break during your working career?

_____

_____

_____

_____

_____

What did you do? _____

_____

_____

_____

_____

_____

_____

_____

_____

_____

_____

_____

_____

Did you have a mentor to guide you in your work?

_____

_____

_____

_____

_____

_____

_____

_____

What kinds of things did you learn from this person?

_____

_____

_____

_____

_____

_____

_____

_____

Overall, have you liked the work that you have done?

_____

_____

_____

_____

_____

_____

_____

_____

_____

_____

_____

_____

_____

_____

_____

_____

_____

_____

_____

_____

_____

If you were to choose another path in life, if you could go back and do it over, what different educational and work choices would you make?

W What other thoughts do you have about work, knowledge, chance, experience, or triumph?

_____

_____

_____

_____

_____

_____

_____

_____

_____

_____

_____

_____

_____

_____

_____

_____

_____

_____

_____

_____

_____

_____

How important is money to you? Why?

_____

_____

_____

_____

_____

_____

_____

_____

_____

_____

Has money made much difference to you in the long run?

_____

_____

_____

_____

_____

_____

_____

_____

_____

_____

_____

W Was money a big concern when choosing a job?

_____

_____

_____

_____

_____

_____

_____

_____

_____

_____

_____

_____

Has there ever been a great investment you could have made but didn't?

_____

_____

_____

_____

_____

_____

_____

_____

_____

_____

_____

Travels

Places	Companions	Dates

W What has traveling meant to you?

_____
_____
_____
_____
_____
_____
_____
_____
_____
_____

How has it shaped you as a person?

_____
_____
_____
_____
_____
_____
_____
_____
_____
_____

What were your best or most memorable vacations or trips?

Who went with you?

W

What were your worst vacations or trips?

_____

_____

_____

_____

_____

_____

_____

_____

_____

_____

Why? _____

_____

_____

_____

_____

_____

_____

_____

_____

What were your favorite places to visit?

Would you want to, or could you, live there all the time?

W Where would you like to go that you haven't been to yet?

_____

_____

_____

_____

_____

_____

_____

_____

_____

_____

Have you ever had an experience while traveling that significantly changed your perspective on life or home? How?

_____

_____

_____

_____

_____

_____

_____

_____

_____

_____

_____

Do you have any special hobbies or passions? What are they?

Do you like to read?

_____

_____

_____

_____

_____

What kinds of books? _____

_____

_____

_____

_____

_____

_____

_____

Who are your favorite authors? _____

_____

_____

_____

_____

_____

Favorite Books of All Time

Book

Author

Summary

Book

Author

Summary

Book

Author

Summary

Other favorite books

D Did any books or stories you read as a kid especially influence you?

_____

_____

_____

_____

_____

_____

_____

_____

_____

_____

If you were to recommend just two books to your future great-great-grandchild, what would they be?

_____

_____

_____

_____

_____

_____

_____

_____

_____

D o you like poetry?

_____

_____

_____

_____

What are your favorite poems?

_____

_____

_____

_____

_____

_____

_____

_____

Who are your favorite poets?

_____

_____

_____

_____

Do you routinely read the newspaper or certain magazines?

_____

_____

_____

Newspaper/Magazine	Why I read it

D o you watch television often?

_____

_____

_____

_____

_____

What are your favorite old radio and television shows?

_____

_____

_____

_____

_____

What are your current favorites?

_____

_____

_____

_____

_____

What major news events do you recall learning about via the radio or television that remain indelible?

_____

_____

_____

_____

Favorite Television Shows of All Time

Television show _____

Actor _____

Actress _____

Why I liked it _____

_____

_____

Television show _____

Actor _____

Actress _____

Why I liked it _____

_____

_____

Television show _____

Actor _____

Actress _____

Why I liked it _____

_____

_____

Other favorite television shows _____

_____

_____

D o you like to watch sports or other competitive events? Which ones?

In person or on television?

What are your favorites?

Do you like to play any sports or games? Which ones?

_____

_____

_____

_____

How often?

_____

_____

_____

_____

_____

_____

Do you have any special achievements?

_____

_____

_____

_____

_____

HOW I SPEND MY TIME

W What memorable sporting events do you recall?

Has competition played a big role in your life?

_____

_____

_____

_____

_____

_____

_____

_____

_____

_____

_____

_____

_____

_____

_____

_____

_____

_____

_____

_____

Do you like to go to the movies?

What are your favorite old movies?

What are your more recent favorites?

Who are your favorite movie actors and actresses?

Favorite Movies of All Time

Movie _____

Actor _____

Actress _____

Why I liked it _____

_____

_____

Movie _____

Actor _____

Actress _____

Why I liked it _____

_____

_____

Movie _____

Actor _____

Actress _____

Why I liked it _____

_____

_____

Other favorite movies _____

_____

_____

Do you like plays? Broadway musicals? Opera? Ballet?

What have been your favorite shows?

D o you enjoy music?

_____

_____

_____

_____

_____

_____

_____

_____

_____

_____

Have you ever played an instrument? Do you still?

_____

_____

_____

_____

_____

_____

_____

_____

_____

_____

_____

HOW I SPEND MY TIME

Favorite Songs of All Time

Song	Artist

What were your favorite songs while growing up?

What songs stir up special memories for you?

D o you like to dance?

_____

_____

_____

_____

_____

What styles of dance?

_____

_____

_____

_____

_____

_____

_____

_____

_____

_____

To what kinds of music?

_____

_____

_____

_____

D Do you enjoy art?

What are your favorite paintings, sculptures, or other pieces?

W Who are your favorite artists?

_____

_____

_____

_____

_____

_____

_____

_____

_____

_____

_____

Who are your favorite photographers?

_____

_____

_____

_____

_____

_____

_____

_____

_____

_____

_____

Do you like to cook?

Do you have a recipe you would like to share?

W What favorite restaurants have you discovered?

_____

_____

_____

_____

_____

_____

_____

_____

_____

_____

_____

What are your favorite dishes?

_____

_____

_____

_____

_____

_____

_____

_____

_____

_____

_____

What else do you do, or have you done in the past, for entertainment?

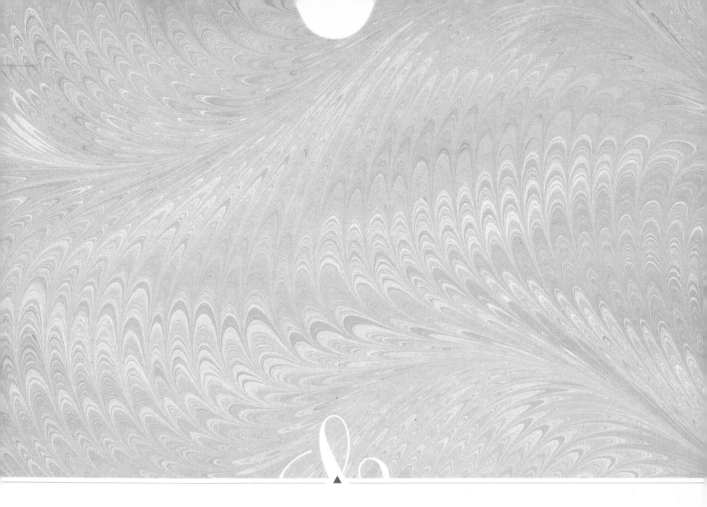

MEMENTOS

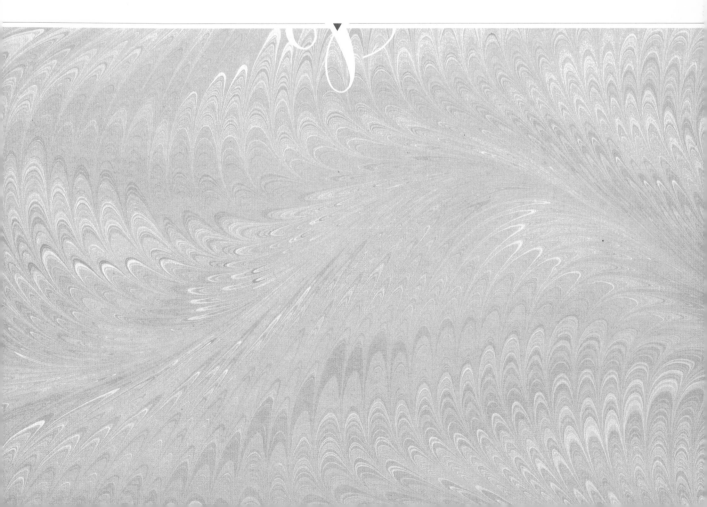

MEMENTOS

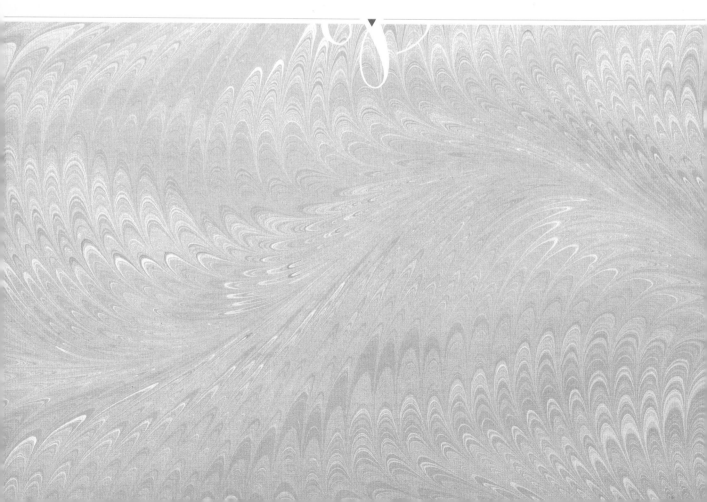

MY BELIEFS AND VALUES

W What is your general view of the world and a human being's place in the universe?

Do you think that people are essentially good or bad? Why?

Do you believe in fate and destiny?

Do you believe in God or a Supreme Being?

_____

_____

_____

_____

_____

_____

_____

_____

_____

_____

_____

_____

_____

_____

_____

_____

_____

_____

Were you raised in a religious environment?

_____

_____

_____

_____

_____

_____

_____

_____

_____

What were your parents' religious beliefs?

_____

_____

_____

_____

_____

_____

_____

_____

_____

Are you actively committed to an organized religious group?

W What has your faith meant to you?

Do you pray? How often?

_____

_____

_____

_____

_____

_____

_____

_____

_____

_____

_____

What have you most frequently prayed about?

_____

_____

_____

_____

_____

_____

_____

_____

_____

_____

_____

D o you believe in life after death?

_____

_____

_____

_____

_____

_____

_____

_____

_____

Have you ever experienced an unexplainable spiritual event? What was it?

_____

_____

_____

_____

_____

_____

_____

_____

_____

_____

Do you believe in heaven?

_____
_____
_____
_____
_____
_____
_____
_____
_____
_____
_____
_____

Do you believe in hell?

_____
_____
_____
_____
_____
_____
_____
_____
_____
_____
_____

What do you think the conditions are for getting into heaven and avoiding hell?

What is the closest that you have come to death? Did it change you? How?

_____

_____

_____

_____

_____

_____

_____

_____

_____

_____

What or who would you die for?

_____

_____

_____

_____

_____

_____

_____

_____

_____

_____

How much value do you place on material things?

I If you were given a million dollars, what would you do with it?

_____

_____

_____

_____

_____

_____

_____

_____

_____

_____

_____

How would you fulfill your dreams?

_____

_____

_____

_____

_____

_____

_____

_____

_____

MY BELIEFS AND VALUES

D Do politics interest you? How?

Do you support a particular political group?

Do you believe in the death penalty? Why or why not?

How have your political views changed over the years?

_____

_____

_____

_____

_____

_____

_____

_____

_____

_____

_____

_____

_____

_____

_____

_____

_____

_____

_____

_____

_____

Who have you most admired in your life?

What about them do you feel is worth emulating?

If you could spend an evening with one or two people—anyone living, historical, or fictional—who would you choose?

_____

_____

_____

_____

_____

_____

_____

_____

_____

What do you think the experience would be like?

_____

_____

_____

_____

_____

_____

_____

_____

MY BELIEFS AND VALUES

Do you recall any quotations that you have enjoyed or that have been meaningful to you?

What do you consider to be your best contribution to the world?

_____

_____

_____

_____

_____

_____

_____

_____

_____

_____

_____

_____

_____

_____

_____

_____

_____

_____

What things about the world frustrate you most? Why?

If you could live to be 150—in good health—would you want to? Why or why not?

What has been your overall experience in life?

LOOKING BACK, LOOKING AHEAD

If you could go back and live your life over again, what would you do differently? Why?

If you could relive a few days of your life, which ones would you choose? Why?

Do you have any regrets?

Are there any apologies you would like to make to someone?

Are there any people you would like to acknowledge or thank for their part in your life? Who? Why?

How would you like to be remembered?

Are there any injustices you have observed or experienced that you wish could have been corrected?

_____

_____

_____

_____

_____

Is it too late?

_____

_____

_____

_____

_____

_____

_____

_____

_____

_____

_____

LOOKING BACK, LOOKING AHEAD

What new inventions and new technologies introduced in your lifetime
do you think were most significant?

_____

_____

_____

_____

_____

_____

_____

_____

_____

_____

_____

_____

_____

_____

_____

_____

_____

_____

_____

_____

_____

If you were given the opportunity to go on a flight into space, would you do it? Why?

_____

_____

_____

_____

_____

_____

_____

_____

_____

_____

_____

_____

_____

_____

_____

_____

_____

_____

What have been the most important or memorable historical events you have witnessed?

Are there any private, personal things about you that those who know you would be surprised to learn?

_____

_____

_____

_____

_____

_____

_____

_____

_____

_____

_____

_____

_____

_____

_____

_____

_____

_____

_____

W Who or what do you miss the most?

W What wishes or fantasies do you still want to have fulfilled?

_____

_____

_____

_____

_____

_____

_____

_____

_____

_____

_____

_____

_____

_____

_____

_____

_____

_____

_____

What other goals do you have?

SCRAPBOOK